JOURNEY INTO CIVILIZATION
THE ZULUS

by Robert Nicholson

CHELSEA JUNIORS
A division of Chelsea House Publishers
New York • Philadelphia

Editorial Consultant: Ian Knight, BA

This edition published 1994 by Chelsea House Publishers, a division of Main Line Book Co.
300 Park Avenue South, New York, N.Y. 10010 by arrangement with Two-Can Publishing Ltd.
This edition copyright © Two-Can Publishing Ltd., 1994

First published in Great Britain in 1992 by Two-Can Publishing Ltd., 346 Old Street, London EC1V 9NQ
Original edition © Two-Can Publishing Ltd 1992

All rights reserved.

3 5 7 9 8 6 4 2

ISBN 0-7910-2710-4
ISBN 0-7910-2734-1 (pbk.)

Printed in Hong Kong by Wing King Tong Co. Ltd.

Photographic credits:
Anthony Bannister Photo Library: p5, p13, p17, (Nigel Dennis) p19;
Bonhams: p9, p15, p22; The Bridgeman Art Library: p23;
Bruce Coleman Ltd (Gerald Cubitt): p6-7; Gerald Cubitt: p30(l), p30(br);
E.T. Archive: p8; Mary Evans Picture Library: p24(r), p30(tr);
Fotomans Index: p10; The Hulton-Deutsch Collection: p24(l);
Ian Knight: p20; Toby: p12
Illustration credits:
Maxine Hamil: cover, p25-29; Micheala Stewart p4-23

Contents

All words that appear in **bold** can be found in the glossary.

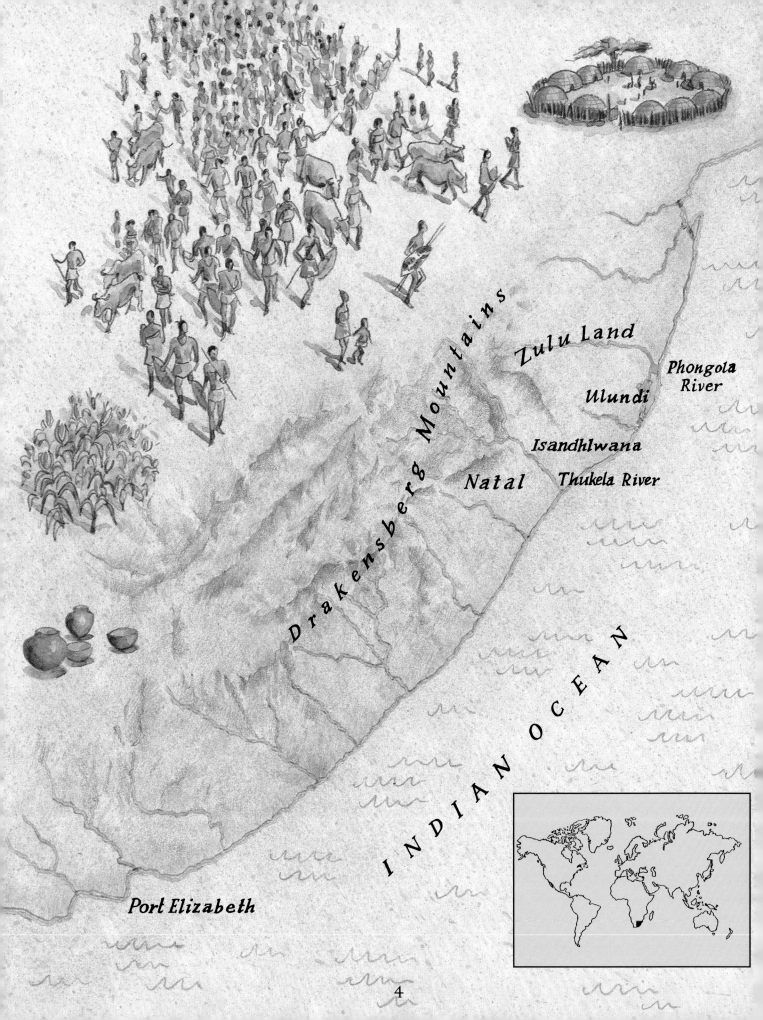

Zulu Land

Phongola River

Ulundi

Drakensberg Mountains

Isandhlwana

Natal

Thukela River

INDIAN OCEAN

Port Elizabeth

The Zulu World

The Zulu people are the descendants of a wandering tribe of cattle-owning warriors. This tribe came to southern Africa from further north hundreds of years before any Europeans arrived in the African continent.

Zulu homelands were originally located between the Phongola and Thukela rivers. Zulus spread from this area, conquering their neighbors, until they became the strongest tribe in this part of Africa. In the nineteenth century, the Zulus were one of the most powerful and organized military forces Africa has ever known. Their bravery was famous throughout the world.

Eventually, however, the Zulus clashed with **immigrants** from Europe who were settling the countryside around Zululand in large numbers. The Zulus fought long and hard to keep their lands but were finally defeated in the war of 1879.

▼ Most Zulu settlements were concentrated in the plains between the Drakensberg mountains and the coast.

Zulu Lands

The homeland of the Zulus was a series of rolling hills and wooded valleys situated between the Drakensberg mountains in the west, and to the east, the marshy coastal plain of the Indian Ocean.

The weather in this area is moderate. Summers are hot and wet, winters cool and dry. The rivers that flow to the ocean provide water and the wide and fertile valleys are covered in rich grasses. Several different types of grass grow all year round. In most parts of Africa the tsetse fly infects and kills the livestock, but it is not found in Zululand.

In fact, the area provides perfect grazing land for cattle the whole year round. The Zulus were ready to fight hard to keep this precious land.

▲ Streams cut across the central plains of the Zulu lands, creating sheltered, well-watered valleys. This landscape is ideal for cattle herding.

Chiefs and Warriors

The Zulus were one of a group of tribes known as the **Nguni.** Each tribe believed that its members were descended from one particular man. The Zulus' ancestor was a man called Zulu.

Each tribe had a chief, or **inkhosi**. He was supported by a body of warriors called an **ibutho**. The ibutho fought for him in war, accompanied him on hunting trips and helped build his homestead. In fact, the young men of the ibutho were considered the property of the chief until they married.

In return, the chief would reward them with cattle and gifts, such as feathers and necklaces of olive wood, for exceptional acts of loyalty and bravery.

Usually tribes fought each other for cattle or for grazing land. They fought with long throwing spears and ox-hide shields. The cattle of each ibutho were the same color, so that all their hide shields were uniform. White shields belonged to the oldest regiment, while the youngest regiment's shields were totally black.

▼ This painting shows King Mpande reviewing his troops. He reigned for 32 years, and was the only Zulu king to die peacefully in old age.

◀ An ox-hide shield. The slits can be seen clearly.

Making Shields

Zulus made their shields out of ox hide. They usually used the hides of males.

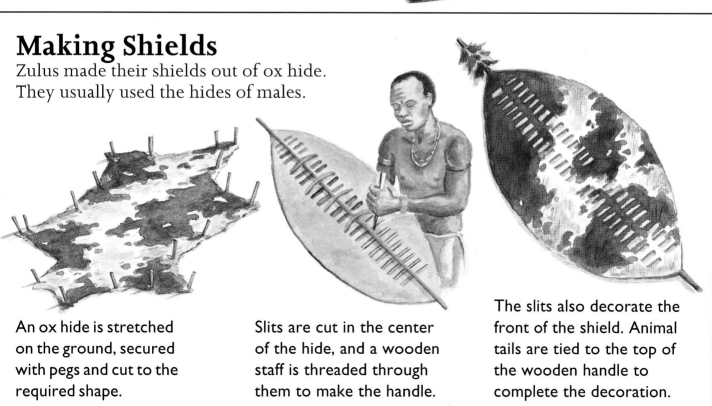

An ox hide is stretched on the ground, secured with pegs and cut to the required shape.

Slits are cut in the center of the hide, and a wooden staff is threaded through them to make the handle.

The slits also decorate the front of the shield. Animal tails are tied to the top of the wooden handle to complete the decoration.

Shaka Zulu

Shaka became inkhosi in 1816. He was a great military leader, and made the Zulus the most powerful of the Nguni people.

He led the Zulus during a series of bloody battles called the **mfecane**. Land for cattle-grazing was becoming hard to find as the population increased, and the Nguni tribes were fighting each other for it.

Shaka introduced new fighting methods and developed new weapons. Boys of the same age were brought together in military camps where they were trained and drilled. Discipline was strict, but bravery in battle was always generously rewarded. The army was made up of regiments, or **impis**. Each had its own war cries, distinctive ox-hide shields and uniforms.

By 1824, Shaka's warriors had defeated most of the rival tribes. Their soldiers joined Shaka's regiments, and some tribes even adopted the name Zulu. Shaka had started with about 400 followers; he now had over 15,000. The victorious Zulus had emerged as the strongest of the Nguni, and Shaka became king of the united tribes.

▼ Shaka, king of the Zulus, in 1825. His uniform is made of monkey skins and cow-tails.

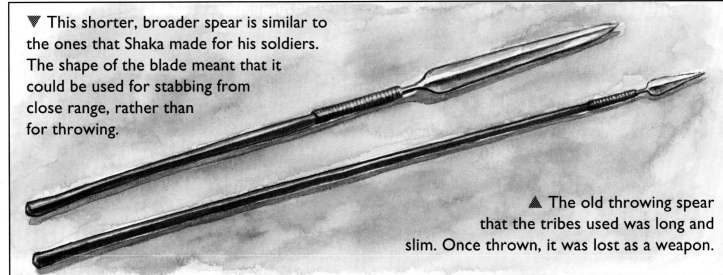

▼ This shorter, broader spear is similar to the ones that Shaka made for his soldiers. The shape of the blade meant that it could be used for stabbing from close range, rather than for throwing.

▲ The old throwing spear that the tribes used was long and slim. Once thrown, it was lost as a weapon.

Impondo Zankomo

The Nguni tribes were used to battles in which not many men were killed and one side gave up quickly. Shaka's army was prepared to fight to the death. Shaka invented a new fighting tactic known as the **impondo zankomo,** or bull's horns. The main body of soldiers would attack the enemy's center, while the "horns" surrounded them on either side. He also persuaded his men to fight without sandals, which allowed them to run much faster.

Shaka also made his men marry much later in life so that they were available to fight for longer. Often they did not marry until they were in their forties.

Crops and Cattle

Cattle were a Zulu's most important possession. A man's wealth was judged by how many cattle he owned. The Zulus had over 300 words just to describe the different colors of their cattle. Each man knew his own cattle so well that even in a huge herd one animal's absence would be noticed at once. As a source of food, cattle were vital, particularly for their milk. Meat was eaten only on special occasions.

While the men tended the cattle, Zulu women grew crops. Each married woman had her own little plot of land. In August and September, the women would start planting by scattering seeds on their plots. Until the summer months of December and January, the crops would be watered, weeded and watched carefully to make sure that birds and small animals did not attack them. Harvesting started in January and continued until May or June. The harvested crops were stored in pits in the ground.

corn

pumpkin

▶ The main crops grown by the Zulus were corn, which they called mealie, sugar cane, pumpkins, root vegetables, watermelon and a sort of grass called sorghum.

sugar cane

sweet potato

watermelon

12

Herds of cattle wandered the grasslands during the day, watched by small boys who frightened away wild animals. At night they were kept in an enclosure inside the village.

Spirits and Sacrifices

The Zulus believed in a god or supreme being who had created the world. He was **Nkulunkulu**, but they did not believe that he had any effect on their everyday life.

Instead it was the **amadlozi**, or spirits of ancestors, who guided their everyday lives and brought good or bad luck. Sacrifices were made to these ancestors to make sure that they looked favorably upon the Zulus.

Ancestors were only seen in dreams, and only **isangomas,** or diviners, had the special powers to be able to communicate with them. They were consulted if a simple sacrifice had failed to bring the desired result. They threw bones and shells on the ground and looked carefully at the pattern they made. This indicated to them the advice they should give. Isangomas wore leopard-skull headdresses and extraordinary clothes, hung with animal skins, bags of animal bones and medicines.

There were also **inyanga,** or herbalists, who used herbs to make remedies for different illnesses.

Talking with the Ancestors

⬤ Zulu diviners always took **snuff** before talking with the ancestors. They believed that snuff cleared their heads, and helped them to hear the ancestors' voices.

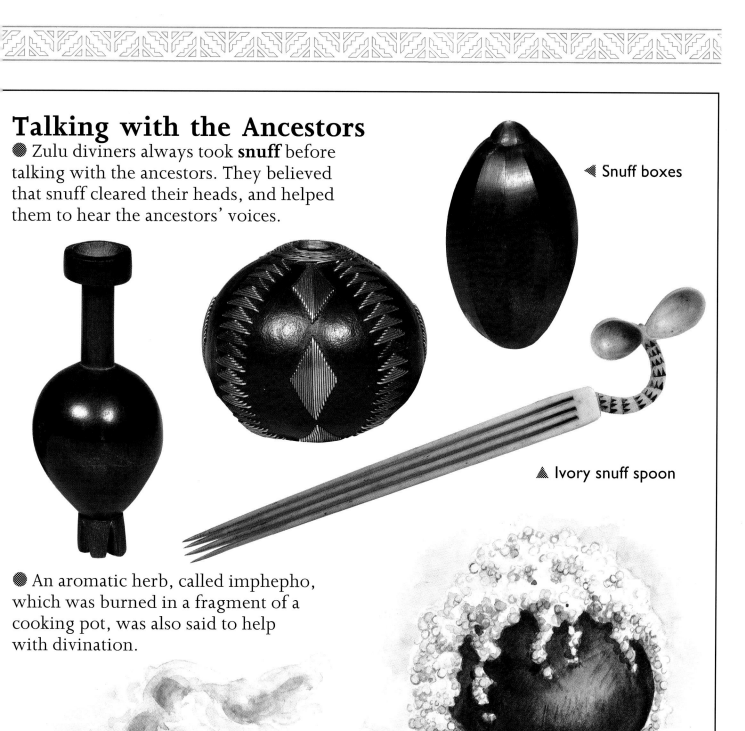

◀ Snuff boxes

▲ Ivory snuff spoon

⬤ An aromatic herb, called imphepho, which was burned in a fragment of a cooking pot, was also said to help with divination.

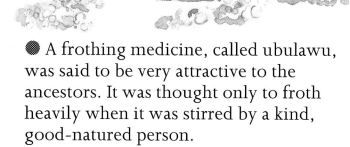

⬤ A frothing medicine, called ubulawu, was said to be very attractive to the ancestors. It was thought only to froth heavily when it was stirred by a kind, good-natured person.

The Umuzi

Zulu families lived in homesteads called **umuzi**. Each umuzi was a group of huts, arranged in a circle and surrounded by a stout fence of posts. In the middle was another enclosure where the cattle could be kept at night. Several umuzi could be built close together to make up a village. Each umuzi was owned by a headman, or **induna**. He lived there with several wives and many children. The first wife was the most important and it was her eldest son who usually took over when his father died. Younger sons eventually married and established their own umuzi.

Huts were arranged in a set order. The headman's hut was opposite the main entrance. His most important wives had the huts nearest to him. Unmarried sons lived near the entrance. The left side of the hut was for women and the right for men, with the hearth in the middle dividing them. Pots, mugs and cooking instruments hung from the walls of each hut. The hut floors were made from clay or cow dung polished until it shone like dark marble.

The huts were made over a framework of stiff poles, which were driven into the ground, bent over to make the beehive shape and then tied together. This framework was covered with large grass mats, overlapping so that the rainwater would run off them. Wind could pass through the hut, keeping it cool and blowing away the smoke from the fire.

Growing up

Members of Zulu families were taught to respect their elders and to consider them superior. The only people treated as equals were those of the same age and sex.

At the age of about seven, children of the same sex were arranged into age-sets. Boys would begin helping their fathers with the cattle herding and their elder brothers with milking. Girls cleaned the huts, collected water and helped their mothers tend the fields. There were no schools, so children learned the skills they needed by helping their parents.

As the Zulus had no form of writing, the children were taught about their tribe's history and customs through storytelling.

Boys often played games which helped teach them the skills of war and fighting.

A popular game was rolling a large melo down a hill, and trying to hit it with spear before it reached the bottom.

At the next stage, at the age of 11 or 12, the boys started to look after the herds on their own, and the girls to cook and look after their baby brothers and sisters.

At the age of 14 or 15, girls could marry. At this age, boys left the umuzi to join thei ibutho, where they remained until they were married. Ambitious young men built up their own herd of cattle, because they had to be able to give their future bride's family a **lobola**, or gift of cattle.

Clothes

Everyday clothing was very simple. Men wore a leather belt with two strips of hide hanging down the front and back. Women often wore a similar outfit or a simple skirt wrapped around the body.

Hairstyles, like clothing, varied according to age and rank. Young girls wore their hair very short. When they reached the age of seven, they could pierce their ears. Married women wore their hair longer, with a tuft, often dyed with red powder, in the middle of their heads. Married men wove their hair through a ring called an **isicoco**, forming a band around their heads.

Warriors had special clothes for battle. Their bodies were almost entirely covered with cows' tails. They wore leopardskin or otterskin headbands with bird's feathers stuck in them. Different colors represented different regiments.

▲ The scarlet and green feathers of the lourie bird were worn in the headbands of the king's favorite regiments.

19

Mealtimes

The food that the Zulus ate was usually very basic. Elaborate meals were only cooked on special occasions or for ceremonies.

The main foods were corn, sorghum, sugar, watermelons and pumpkins, eaten with **amasi,** or curdled milk. A sour grey beer was also made from millet. There were usually two meals a day, the first at eleven or twelve in the morning, after the cows were milked, and the main meal in the evening, when the day's work was finished.

Important Occasions

● For important occasions, special food was prepared. An **umkhosi**, or harvest festival, was held in December or January when fruit and vegetables were ripe and ready. Before the feast, a bull was captured and wrestled to the ground by members of a top regiment. The roasted flesh of the bull was thought to be good medicine.

● A bull was also killed before major battles, and was fed to the whole army in tiny strips of meat.

Good manners were very important at Zulu meals. Hands and faces were carefully washed before the meal. The men of the family sat on the right of the hut, with the eldest nearest the door, and the women on the other side. It was thought very rude to sit on the bare floor of the hut, so each person had his or her own reed mat to sit on. A big dish of boiled corn, roasted corn cobs or sweet potatoes was set in the center of the group. Spoons were set around the dish with their handles on the floor and their bowls on the rim.

▲ Food was stored in raised huts to protect it from animals and from the damp.

21

Crafts

The Zulus' skill in arts and crafts was shown through the decoration of everyday things. The men were skilled woodcarvers, and used small iron knives and choppers to make beautiful pots, plates, combs and spoons. They even made wooden pillows, which protected their elaborate hairstyles while they slept. Other household utensils were made from bone or ivory.

Zulu women were expert weavers. Some baskets were so tightly woven they could hold a liquid, like beer. They also used clay to make pottery. The Zulus had no pottery wheels so the clay was rolled out into a long snake shape and then wound around to make the pot. A sharp stone was used to smooth the surface of a pot. The clay was then dried in the sun or near a small fire.

▶ Wooden staffs, or walking sticks, carved into the shapes of male and female figures.

Bead Codes

The Zulus made decorative beads from cowrie and ostrich shells and polished wood. When glass beads were introduced by the first traders from Europe, the Zulus began to weave them into all sorts of everyday goods and into their clothes. They began using different colors to represent emotions or meanings, usually about love and courtship, and sent each other messages through the beads.

▲ Many colored beads have been woven into this decorated belt.

(blue) = loyal and true

(black) = marriage

(white) = my heart, purity

(gray-blue) = send a message

(green) = young

(pink) = poor

You could try this yourself with friends. Decide what each color will mean and then string together necklaces, so you can send messages without speaking or writing a word!

▲ This necklace is sending the following message: "My heart is pure, but you are young and poor. When will you send me a message that you can pay my bride price? Then my heart will be yours, and I will be loyal and true."

The Zulu Wars

The Zulu way of life was shattered by the Zulu War of 1879. Zulus had clashed with white settlers in small battles for fifty years, but this war was their final defeat.

In 1879, British colonists decided that they needed more farmland for their growing colonial population. They saw the Zulus as an obstacle to this and organized an invasion. The British army entered Zululand but was surprised by the Zulus at Isandlwana. The Zulus surrounded the British troops and inflicted a crushing defeat, which brought the war to the attention of the rest of the world. At the final battle of Ulundi, the British used modern weapons, including machine guns, to destroy the Zulu army. The British captured Cetshwayo, the Zulu king, and took him back to London.

As many as 20,000 Zulu warriors were killed in battle, which meant that their army could not become powerful again for many years. When they did rise up again in 1906, the Zulus' brave traditions could not protect them against the colonists' modern weapons.

▲ This lantern slide shows Cetshwayo's warriors in a circular war dance.

◀ An early photograph of King Cetshwayo, defeated by the British in the Zulu wars.

The King of the Birds

The Zulus told many tales about spirits and about the world around them.
This tale tries to explain why the owl sleeps during the day
and wakes up at night.

We all know that the lion is the king of the beasts. One day, however, the birds decided that there should be a king of the birds. They all came to a great meeting to decide who deserved the title. The eagle was there, and the vulture. The weaver bird came and so did the ostrich and the flamingo and the secretary bird. In fact every single kind of bird you can possibly think of was there, even the ones that have no names at all.

The birds quarreled and bickered, trying to decide who should be king. The ostrich thought he should be king, because he was so big. The flamingo thought he should be king, because of his beautiful pink color.

The weaver bird thought he deserved the crown, because he was so clever. They talked for hours, until the shadows grew long and the sun was low in the sky.

"I know," shouted the little ox-pecker. "Let's have a contest. The bird who can fly the highest shall be the king!"

All the birds thought this was a wonderful idea, except the ostrich and a few other birds, who were disqualified for not being able to fly. It was decided that the contest would start tomorrow, at dawn.

To make him feel better about not joinin in, the ostrich was given the job of starting the contest. So, the next morning, he made all the birds stand in a long line...

"GO!" he shouted, and was surrounded by a tremendous fluttering of wings.

From the first moment it was obvious who would win. As the other birds fluttere about, the eagle pulled himself through the air with his strong wings. He soared highe

nd higher, and all the other birds
adually gave up and came back down to
e ground.

"And the winner is…" the ostrich began.
But he was forced to stop. Suddenly
veryone spotted another bird. As the eagle
arted to tire and to return to the ground, a
ny brown bird was visible still struggling
rther upwards.

"How did he get there?" they wondered.
As the little bird and the eagle flew back
wn to the ground, the other birds began
cheer and stamp their feet.

"Hurray for the little bird! Hurray for
our new king!"

"Wait a minute!" shouted the eagle as
soon as he had caught his breath. "He's a
cheat. He hid underneath the feathers on
my neck until I had flown as high as I could
go; then he flew on above my head."

"Rules are rules," said the ostrich.

"We said whichever bird flew the highest

would be king. We did not say that he had to fly all the way!"

"Rubbish," said the secretary bird. "He's a cheat, and should be punished."

All the other birds agreed. The eagle said nothing, but kept his beady eyes pinned on the cheat and now and then scratched the ground with his sharp talons. The eagle's gaze was making the little bird feel very uncomfortable. Suddenly he flew off and disappeared down a nearby hole in the ground.

"What are we going to do now?" wailed the flamingo, fluttering his pink feathers.

"We will have to guard the hole until he comes out," replied the secretary bird.

The owl was chosen to keep a lookout because he had such big eyes. The other birds went back to their nests to sleep. Owl stood up straight, watching the hole. After a while, he grew a bit stiff, so he hopped from foot to foot.

Then he began to get sleepy. First he closed one eye, and then he opened that one and closed the other. Then, he started all over again. At last, he blinked, and both of his eyes closed.

From the depths of the hole, a tiny head peeked out. Seeing the owl asleep, the little bird crept out of the hole and flew away.

As dawn broke, the other birds returned.

"Owl is asleep!" shouted the ostrich.

"Asleep? What nonsense," said the owl, opening his eyes and shaking himself.

"I just closed my eyes for a few minutes."

"A few minutes too long!" said the flamingo, poking his head down the hole. "The little bird has gone!"

All the birds were furious with the owl for letting the cheat escape. He was so ashamed of himself that he never showed his face in the daytime again.

After all this trouble, the birds never did get around to choosing a king!

How We Know

Have you ever wondered how we know so much about the Zulus when they did not write anything about themselves?

Evidence from the Zulus

There are still around 4 million Zulus in South Africa today. Although many now live in cities, some still live in the country following the traditional ways. Many Zulus remember the **folklore** that makes up their history and tell ancient stories to their children and grandchildren. This give us a good idea of their everyday life in the past.

▲ A lantern slide made during the Zulu War shows Europeans watching Zulu blacksmiths forging an iron spear.

▲ Zulu women load up grain at a trading post in South Africa.

Evidence from the Ground

Archaeologists can investigate battle sites to see how a battle took place, or how many men died. Remains of Zulu campsites can indicate how many men a chief commanded. Discoveries of Zulu weapons show how spears were made. Homesteads of the great kings, such as Cetshwayo, have been examined and reconstructed.

Evidence from the Colonis

British and Dutch immigrants wrote about Zulus they encountered, but their accounts were often inaccurate. The immigrants thought the Zulus' simple way of life was uncivilized. Some writers, such as John Colenso, Bishop of Natal, wrote accurately and sympathetically about the Zulus.

▲ Many Zulus still live in the traditional way in villages of thatched "beehive" huts.

Glossary

amadlozi
The ancestor spirits who could bring good or bad luck.

amasi
A curdled milk drink.

folklore
The tales passed down through generations of people, which may be based on real events.

butho
A body of warriors who fought and hunted for a chief.

immigrant
A foreign person who settles in a country.

impi
A regiment in the Zulu army.

impondo zankomo
The bull's horns formation used in battle.

induna
A headman.

inkhosi
A tribal chief.

inyanga
A person with a knowledge of medicine and healing.

isangoma
A person with special powers who communicates with the amadlozi.

isicoco
A ring used for dressing a man's hair.

lobola
A gift of cattle given to a new wife's family on her marriage.

mfecane
The series of battles in which Shaka led the Zulus against the other Nguni tribes.

Nguni
The group of tribes to which the Zulus belonged.

Nkulunkulu
The Zulu god who was believed to have created the world.

snuff
Powdered tobacco which is sniffed up the nostrils.

umkhosi
A harvest festival which usually took place in December or January.

umuzi
A homestead.

Index